LET'S VISIT THE SOUTH PACIFIC

LET'S VISIT THE SOUTH PACIFIC
FIJI-TONGA-TAHITI

Since they were first discovered by European sea captains and explorers the islands of the South Pacific have fascinated all who saw them. Many artists and writers, including Herman Melville, Robert Louis Stevenson and Paul Gauguin, have visited the islands, fallen under their spell and decided to live there. An American author, James Michener, wrote a best-selling novel about them called *Tales of the South Pacific* which was later made into the popular play and movie. *Mutiny on the Bounty,* a historical novel, also made into a movie, tells an exciting sea story — based on fact — which takes place in waters surrounding Tahiti and the Tongas.

There are over two thousand islands scattered in the Pacific Ocean, from Australia to our own Hawaii, in an area 1,200 miles on either side of the equator. Some of the islands were once used by European countries as naval bases, but now they are of little military or economic importance. Westerners, however, still find their histories, cultures and startling beauty interesting.

John C. Caldwell visited the South Pacific twice in 1962. In this book Mr. Caldwell tells us of the geography, the history and the people of the major island groups — the Fijis (from which the Tongas and Pitcairn Island are administered) and the islands of French Polynesia, of which Tahiti in the Society group is the main island and perhaps the best known of any South Pacific Island.

Let's Visit the South Pacific

Fiji — Tonga — Tahiti

JOHN C. CALDWELL

The John Day Company, New York

By John C. Caldwell

LET'S VISIT AMERICANS OVERSEAS
LET'S VISIT ARGENTINA
LET'S VISIT AUSTRALIA
LET'S VISIT BRAZIL
LET'S VISIT CANADA
LET'S VISIT CENTRAL AMERICA
LET'S VISIT CEYLON
LET'S VISIT CHILE
LET'S VISIT CHINA
LET'S VISIT COLOMBIA
LET'S VISIT FORMOSA
LET'S VISIT INDIA
LET'S VISIT INDONESIA
LET'S VISIT JAPAN
LET'S VISIT KOREA (With Elsie F. Caldwell)
LET'S VISIT MEXICO
LET'S VISIT MIDDLE AFRICA
LET'S VISIT THE MIDDLE EAST
LET'S VISIT NEW ZEALAND
LET'S VISIT PAKISTAN
LET'S VISIT PERU
LET'S VISIT THE PHILIPPINES
LET'S VISIT SOUTHEAST ASIA
LET'S VISIT THE SOUTH PACIFIC
LET'S VISIT VENEZUELA
LET'S VISIT VIETNAM
LET'S VISIT WEST AFRICA
LET'S VISIT THE WEST INDIES

Data in this book brought up-to-date 1966

Third Impression

Library of Congress Catalogue Card Number: 63-10229

MANUFACTURED IN THE UNITED STATES OF AMERICA

Contents

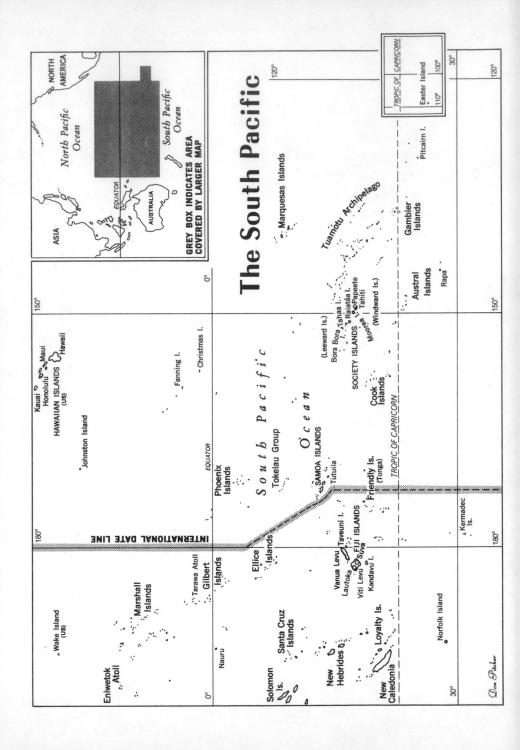

The South Pacific

GREY BOX INDICATES AREA
COVERED BY LARGER MAP

Let's Visit the South Pacific

For hundreds of years the islands of the South Pacific have captured the imagination of sailors. When I visited the islands in 1962, I saw sailboats out of Honolulu, Los Angeles, San Diego — even far away Bridgeport, Connecticut. On one of the sailboats there was a family with three small children, all brown as nuts from days in the sun.

Famous writers and painters have gone to visit the South Pacific Islands. Often, because of the beauty of the islands and the mysteries surrounding their peoples, the visits have turned into years of living among them. Herman Melville, author of the book *Moby Dick,* lived in the Marquesas (pronounced Mar-KAY-zas) Islands. Robert Louis Stevenson lived on Tahiti and in Samoa. Several best-selling books have been written about the islands. *Tales of the South Pacific,* by an American writer named James Michener, was

9

made into one of the most successful musical plays of all time.

Let's take a look at the map and locate the islands of the Pacific. The Hawaiian Islands are the most northerly of the Pacific Islands. South of Hawaii there are only a few tiny islands and coral reefs for over 1,000 miles. Among these are Johnston Island and Christmas Island, where our government has carried out thermonuclear testing.

Easter Island, belonging to Chile in South America, lies far to the east of the South Pacific Islands we will read about in this book. On the western side of the Pacific, the islands extend almost to Australia and to New Guinea, one of the world's largest islands.

The islands we will visit stretch across an area north of Australia and New Zealand to our own Hawaiian Islands. There are hundreds of islands, many uninhabited. Most of them are found in an area 1,200 miles on either side of the equator. It is this area that we call the South Pacific.

We will first visit the Fiji Islands, a British Crown Colony located 1,300 miles east of Australia. The Fiji group is the largest and most populated of the South Pacific Islands.

Southeast of the Fijis are the Friendly or Tonga Islands, ruled by a queen, as a British protectorate. To the north of the Tonga Islands are the Samoa Islands. Western Samoa has recently become independent, after many years of protection under New Zealand. The small islands of eastern Samoa, with a population of only 20,000, are a territory of the United States.

Finally, almost 2,000 miles east of the Fiji Islands, we find the many island groups that make up French Polynesia. These islands lying over 3,000 miles south of Hawaii, include the Society Islands, the Austral Islands, the Tuamotu Archipelago and the Marquesas Islands. Tahiti is the best-known island of the French Polynesian group and perhaps the best known of all South Pacific Islands.

The total population of the islands we will visit in this book is about 600,000, or less than the population of Pittsburgh or New Orleans.

These islands are not very important from an economic standpoint. There are some mineral resources and coconuts, vanilla beans and some sugar are produced, but not much else.

In olden days the United States and the seafaring nations of Europe wanted good and safe harbors for use as naval bases. At the time when European explorers were looking for the spices and riches of the East Indies, it was thought that the Pacific Islands might also be areas of great wealth.

During World War II the islands were important to our country and our allies. Many thousands of American soldiers were stationed in the Fiji Islands and the islands of French Polynesia. The islands were important supply bases and jumping-off places for American attacks against Japanese-held islands.

Although the islands are no longer militarily important, they are still very interesting. They have a history of battle and bloodshed. Before the coming of European explorers

The grave of a Fiji cannibal chief

and traders, the island people fought and ate one another. Then they fought and often ate white men! On Viti Levu in the Fiji Islands, I saw the grave of a Fijian chief. Around the grave were nine hundred round stones. Each stone represented one human being eaten by the chief.

There are unsolved mysteries as to where the island people came from. There are unusual customs, and scenery as beautiful as may be found anywhere in the world.

The United States has played an important part in the history and development of the South Pacific Islands. American sailing ships from New England visited the islands; American traders settled on some of them. At one time many residents of the Fiji Islands petitioned the President of the United States to annex the islands.

Reached only by long ship voyages a few years ago, there is now direct nonstop air service from Los Angeles to Papeete (pronounced Pah-pay-AY-tay), capital of the many islands of French Polynesia. Planes from Honolulu can reach the Fiji Islands, Samoa and Tahiti, within a few hours. Thousands of American tourists are visiting the islands of the Pacific each year.

In this book we will learn about the history, geography and peoples of the South Pacific. First we will learn about the unusual geography of the islands.

High Islands and Low Islands

As much as scientists know about the earth, there are still mysteries. We can only guess at some aspects of the earth millions of years ago. We know that Asia and North America were connected where we now have the Bering Strait. Perhaps the large islands north of Australia were connected with the mainland of Asia.

The main area of the Pacific Ocean was open sea. All through the South Pacific there was a period of volcanic activity. Great eruptions from the ocean floor pushed masses of rock and lava above the surface of the water. In this way islands were scattered across the Pacific.

The Hawaiian Islands are the most northerly of these volcanic islands. Mauna Loa, 13,680 feet high, is the world's largest active volcano.

As we read about the geography of the Pacific Islands we will use several descriptive words. One of these is the term "high island." Islands produced by volcanic action are high islands. Moorea Island, in French Polynesia, is a high island. There are many mountains, some quite high. Some of the peaks are jagged, and there are high cliffs.

On this page there is also a picture of Viti Levu, largest of the Fiji Islands. It too is a high island. However, the mountains of Viti Levu are more rounded and are not as high. This island and many others in the South Pacific are high islands, but they also are *old* islands. The volcanic eruptions which formed the islands occurred very long ago.

Viti Levu in the Fiji Islands

Moorea is a high island.

Rain and wind have caused erosion, and the mountains have become rounded and lowered. In our country we have the Appalachian ranges of mountains in the east and the Rocky Mountains in the west. The former are older and lower than the younger Rockies.

The new high islands of the Pacific were formed by volcanic action that took place millions of years ago. The low high islands are even older. The islands of the Tahiti group are new high islands, with the highest peak having an elevation of 7,350 feet. The Fiji Islands are older, the highest point being about 4,300 feet in elevation.

15

In the distance is a low island formed by coral.

On this page there is a picture of a small, low island. There are hundreds of low islands that rise only a few feet above the sea. Low islands are formed by the skeletons of millions of little sea creatures called *polyps*, found only in warm seas. The millions of skeletons harden and gradually push upward from the ocean floor. After millions of years, the hard mass of skeleton pushes itself above the surface of the water.

We use the word *coral* for this hard, rocklike mass of skeletons. When coral pushes above the ocean surface, a *reef* is formed. In time the reef gets higher and wider, and a tiny island comes into being. The word *atoll* (pronounced AT-all) is also used to describe the low, almost completely flat, islands created by coral.

Polyps are still reproducing themselves by the billions, are still dying, and are forming new coral. Atolls and most of the high islands are surrounded by rings of coral. Sometimes this circle of coral reef pushes just above the surface; sometimes it is below the surface. The coral reefs around some islands — as in the case of Tutuila, American Samoa — are close to the island shore. But there are parts of Viti Levu where the reef is so far offshore it cannot be seen.

We use the words *barrier reef* for the rings of coral surrounding the islands of the Pacific. We might think of the reefs as new islands being formed. Often there are small islands as a part of a reef. Usually the barrier reefs are within a few hundred yards to a mile or two from the islands they surround.

The water between the barrier reefs and the islands is called a *lagoon* (pronounced la-GOON). Lagoon waters are shallow and calm. The high waves of the open sea break against the barrier reefs and cannot rush through and against the shore. On this page there is a picture of a typical barrier reef. We can see the white crest of the waves breaking over the reef. The water between the reef and the shoreline is calm and protected.

Here and there in almost every barrier reef there are breaks or open spaces leading into the lagoons. Ever since the islands were formed and were inhabited, men have used these gaps in the reefs to reach the safety of the lagoons. But there have been many cases of ships which did not find the opening and which were wrecked upon the jagged coral reefs. The first peoples of the islands were often wrecked; the early European explorers often ran aground and were wrecked. When I visited Viti Levu, largest island of the Fiji group, I saw a large Japanese fishing boat which had crashed and been wrecked on the barrier reef. Every year there are wrecks, either because ships' captains do not know the location of the openings leading into safe water, or because storms drive their ships against the reefs.

Sometimes the barrier reef is close to shore.

AUTHOR

Coral is of several colors. There is red coral, black coral, white coral. The different colors produce beautiful effects, not only along the reefs but in the lagoons as well. The color of the water is partly determined by the color and amount of coral scattered through the lagoons. The waters just inside the barrier reefs around the Pacific Islands are often visited by skin divers. Even without goggles, we can see the beauties of coral, the numerous brightly colored tropical fish — starfish that are often a bright blue in color — and many varieties of brightly colored shells.

We can understand that the barrier reefs protect the shores of the islands. The calm waters of lagoons provide safe places for boats, fishing and swimming. Sharks, which are common in the South Seas, rarely get into a lagoon.

The land area of high islands averages much larger than the area of low islands. Sometimes an island is almost all lagoon and no land. Eniwetok Atoll, administered as a United Nations trust area by the United States, has a lagoon over twenty miles across. The wide lagoon is surrounded by a circle of reefs. Here and there the reef has pushed above the surface of the water, to form small islands.

There are other islands where there is almost as much water area in the lagoons as land area in the islands. Among these are Christmas Island, where our government tested thermonuclear bombs in 1962; Tarawa Atoll, site of one of World War II's fiercest battles; Wake Island where another battle was fought.

Now we have learned about how the Pacific Islands were formed. We know there are high islands divided among old and new islands and that other islands are known as low islands or atolls. Now let's learn how life came to these islands, many of which are much younger than other parts of the world.

Beginning of Life on the Islands

Except for bats, there were no native animals on the South Pacific Islands. This will show us how separated these islands are from the continents of Australia, Asia and South America. The most common birds on several of the islands were brought there from Asia during the past seventy-five years.

When the islands were formed, there was no life. The low islands were masses of hard, rocklike coral. The high islands consisted of hardened lava and great masses of rock that had been thrown upward from the ocean floor. There was no soil, no plant, bird or animal life.

We use the word *erosion* to describe how soil is eaten away by wind and rain. Rock also can be eroded. After centuries of wind and rain, rock is ground into smaller and smaller particles. There are many different chemicals in this ground-up rock. These chemicals can provide the food needed for plant life. Plants need rainwater too.

We know that there are sea birds that travel long distances

Coconut palms are found on all the islands.

and that many land birds cover thousands of miles in migration. In time, sea birds stopped on the new islands to rest; migrating birds also used the islands as resting places. Occasionally the birds dropped seeds that had caught in their feathers while they were visiting other islands or the mainland where there were trees, bushes and flowers.

In this way, vegetation came to the new islands. And in time some birds decided to live on the islands, to build their nests and raise their young. A few birds were driven by storms from places far away — perhaps Asia or Australia.

21

As the centuries passed, the islands were gradually covered with vegetation. The coconut palm became the common tree of the larger low islands and of the lower places on the high islands. The breadfruit tree became common on the high islands. On many of the small, low islands there is soil only for bushes and low trees. On other islands there are very large trees. The islands of French Polynesia, including Tahiti, Moorea and Bora Bora, have palm trees all along the shores and for a short distance up the mountain slopes. Then the palm trees stop, and we find other trees, many bushes and grass.

Some islands are covered with jungles. The larger islands of the Fiji group have coconut palms near the shore. Within a mile or so the jungle begins, so thick that one cannot move through it without cutting a path. The southern side of Viti Levu, in the Fiji Islands, has perhaps the thickest jungle in the world. There are many kinds of palms, huge hardwoods, ferns as tall as trees. And almost every tree is covered with vines.

But the mountains on the north side of Viti Levu have thick growth only here and there. Often the mountain slopes are covered with grass, ferns and bushes. This is because rainfall plays a large part in the type of vegetation found on an island. There are winds that blow across the Pacific in the same general direction. These are called *trade winds*. The winds pick up moisture as they blow across the ocean. When a moisture-filled cloud strikes a mountain range, there is rainfall.

The prevailing trade winds in the Fiji Islands area strike the southern side of Viti Levu, and rainfall averages more than 120 inches each year. On the other, or northern side of the island, there are only 50 to 60 inches of rain a year. We have the same condition in the United States. The winds that strike our Pacific Coast come across the ocean from the west. When these winds, filled with moisture picked up over the ocean, strike the coastal ranges, there is heavy rainfall. On the other side of the same mountains we find some of our western deserts.

The winds of the Pacific have created another word used to describe islands. In a group of islands there are some known as windward islands, others known as leeward islands. The windward islands are those directly in the path of the prevailing winds. The word leeward is often used for the side of a ship away from the point from which the wind blows. In the same way, a leeward island is one away from, or protected from, the wind.

As we have read, trees, bushes and other vegetation began to grow on the islands of the Pacific. As the rivers were formed, there were fish — their eggs brought in on the legs of shore birds. Bird life began to appear, but there were far fewer different kinds of birds than are found on our continents. Tahiti and the other islands of the Society group have very few native birds. The most common bird on these islands and on several others was brought in by man from Asia. The islands nearer Australia or Asia have more varieties of native birds than do the other islands.

How would animals get to the Pacific Islands? Except for the animals brought in by man, there are very few native animals on the islands. In the Fiji Islands, the only native animal — other than mice and rats, which were probably brought by man centuries ago — is a huge bat called a flying fox. I do not know of *any* native animal in the Society Islands.

There are fewer different kinds of birds and animals in the islands of the Pacific than in any other part of the world.

Now we come to one of the most interesting things about the islands. When, and from what direction, did human beings come? This is one of the scientific puzzles of our world. The peoples of the islands had no written language, and therefore there is no history in writing. There are three distinct types of people in the South Pacific. Although most scientists are in general agreement about the movement of these peoples, there are others who disagree.

Some experts believe the people of the South Pacific came from South America. Experiments have been made that are supposed to prove this. Some of the island people are thought to have come from Northern and Central Asia, through Japan and southward into the Pacific. Others are believed to have come from Central Asia, or from as far away as Africa, through Southeast Asia, and finally to the islands.

In the next section we will read about the different peoples of the South Pacific and the different theories as to when and from what part of the world they came.

The People of the Islands

As we have said, the island people had no written language. The history of different groups and tribes was passed down from generation to generation in the form of songs and legends. In the case of the Fijian people, there was no knowledge of events before the year 1800. We might say that the people of the South Pacific have no history.

We know that South America was inhabited by numerous Indian tribes. There were dark-skinned people living in Australia when it was discovered by Europeans. And people have lived in the islands of Indonesia for thousands of years.

Let's look at the map of the South Pacific. Although widely separated, there are islands between South America and the main South Pacific island groups. We will find Easter Island, then Pitcairn Island. The islands of French Polynesia begin a few hundred miles west of Pitcairn Island. Could the people of the islands have originated in South America?

On the western side of the South Pacific there are many islands. New Guinea is a large island to the north of Australia. Other large islands extend eastward and southeast from New Guinea to within 1,000 miles of the Fiji group.

If the people came from Asia through the large islands, might they not be Asiatic in appearance? Or if the migrations of people came from South America, we might expect the island people to look like American Indians.

However, the people do not look like either Asians or

Indians. Furthermore, they are not all alike in appearance. There are three different racial groups, as well as people who are a mixture of these groups. First, we find a people called *Melanesians*. These people have very dark skins; their hair is *frizzly*. The peoples of the Fiji Islands are Melanesians, as are those of the larger islands near Australia.

Another racial group is called *Polynesian*. These people have light-brown skin and long, wavy or straight hair. The Polynesians often have European facial features.

We have used a small map to show the parts of the Pacific inhabited by each racial group. The Polynesians are found in the eastern islands of the Fiji group and in the Tonga Islands 500 miles southeast of Fiji. All the people east of these islands are Polynesians. And to the north, the Polynesian people are found in the Ellice Islands.

North of the Ellice Islands and all through the many islands of the Western Pacific is a third racial group called the *Micronesians*. The Micronesians are dark-skinned but not as dark as the Melanesians. Their hair is straight. They have some features similar to those of Chinese and Japanese.

In 1947 a Norwegian named Thor Heyerdahl tried an experiment to prove that the Polynesians came from South America. In a small raft named the *Kon Tiki* he and his companions set sail from the coast of Peru. Using only ocean currents and prevailing winds, they crossed 4,300 miles to the Tuamotu Islands.

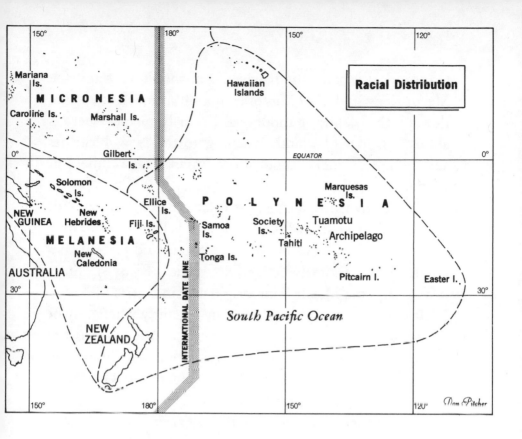

Racial Distribution

150° 180° 150° 120°

Mariana Is.
MICRONESIA
Hawaiian Islands
Caroline Is.   Marshall Is.
Gilbert Is.
EQUATOR 0°
Solomon Is.
Ellice Is.
P O L Y N E S I A
Marquesas Is.
NEW GUINEA   New Hebrides   Fiji Is.
Samoa Is.   Society Is.   Tuamotu
MELANESIA   Tahiti   Archipelago
New Caledonia
AUSTRALIA   Tonga Is.
30°   Pitcairn I.   Easter I.   30°
INTERNATIONAL DATE LINE
South Pacific Ocean
NEW ZEALAND

Don Pitcher

Heyerdahl and some other scientists believe that the Polynesians must have originated in South America. They think that, centuries ago, people sailed from the coast of Peru. The winds and currents brought these people to the islands of Polynesia. Then why do the Polynesions not look like South American Indians? Also there are few similarities in language. For these reasons, most anthropologists — the scientists who study the development of man — do not agree with Heyerdahl's theory.

27

Instead, it is generally believed that the Polynesians, the Melanesians and the Micronesians all came from Asia, through the islands of Indonesia. From Indonesia, there is almost a bridge of islands reaching to the New Hebrides and New Caledonia, about 1,000 miles west of the Fiji Islands.

The Melanesians are thought to be a mixed people with characteristics of the white, black and yellow races. There are some similarities in Fijian place names and place names around Lake Tanganyika in East Africa. Some scientists believe that the Melanesians originated in Africa.

However, no one knows with any certainty where any of the people originated or by what method they reached the Malay Peninsula of Asia and the islands of Indonesia. There probably were several waves of migration. Gradually people reached islands farther and farther away from Asia. Each succeeding migration of people passed on to islands farther east and northeast. In this way the islands were finally populated by Melanesians, Polynesians and those farthest away, the Micronesians.

The Melanesians may have come originally from Africa. Perhaps the Polynesians were a white people who found their way into Southern Asia and finally into the Pacific. And although some scientists believe the Micronesians sailed south and east from Asia, it is more probable that they too used the bridge of islands, beginning at the tip of the Malay Peninsula.

There are Polynesian and Melanesian legends about how

and when the voyages into the Pacific occurred. We know these peoples must have been expert sailors. Of course many may have accidentally drifted to faraway islands. Thousands of people probably lost their lives in Pacific storms.

It is thought that the migrations took place between the first and fifth centuries, during which period the Fiji Islands were reached and settled. Some of the people pushed on to the east. Other migrations are thought to have sailed through the Caroline and Gilbert islands, which are a part of Micronesia. Eventually these explorers reached Tahiti.

Whether they came by way of Fiji or by a more northerly route, the Polynesians of Tahiti began a series of even longer voyages about 700 years ago. From Tahiti they sailed north, south and east in their double-hulled canoes. In this way they reached the Hawaiian Islands and settled there. In the east, the Tuamotu, Pitcairn and Easter islands were discovered.

The Polynesian explorers also discovered a new land far to the south. It is believed the island explorers guessed there was a large land mass to the south, because of the annual migrations of the long-tailed cuckoo. These are land birds that migrate southward from the islands of Polynesia. By following the birds, the Polynesians from Tahiti discovered a land they called Aotearoa (pronounced au-tah-ah-row-a), meaning the Long White Cloud. This is a good name for New Zealand with its high, snow-covered mountains.

During the period from 1300 to 1500, the colonizers

sailed from Tahiti in great fleets of canoes. They completed the colonization of New Zealand and Hawaii. The Maoris of New Zealand are the descendants of these pioneers.

We know that the later voyages were deliberate and not by chance. The canoe fleets took with them breadfruit and banana seedlings, yams and taro plants, dogs, pigs and chickens.

Not including the people of New Guinea, there are perhaps 300,000 Melanesians living in the South Pacific now. Not including the few pure-blooded Polynesians of Hawaii or the Maoris of New Zealand, there are about 250,000 Polynesians in the South Pacific.

In the eighteenth and nineteenth centuries European explorers went to the South Pacific. Soon afterward the Chinese began to go there, and today they are the shopkeepers of the Pacific. Still later, thousands of people were brought in from India, until they finally outnumbered the Melanesians in the Fiji Islands.

Now we come to the period of discovery by European explorers.

Exploration and Discovery

When the first spices were brought to Europe from Asia, European sea captains began voyages of discovery that changed the world's history. Pepper, nutmeg, cinnamon and other spices first came overland. It was known that many spices came from islands to the southeast of India.

It was thought that great treasures would also be found in India and other parts of Asia.

Exploration of the South Pacific and discovery of its islands came as a part of the many voyages made to find a quick and short way of reaching the Spice Islands, also called the Molucca Islands, in the Netherland Indies. In 1520, Magellan sailed through the straits now named for him and on into the Pacific. He passed through, but probably did not see any of, the South Pacific Islands. Magellan did discover Guam, the largest island in the Marianas group, located in the Western Pacific.

Over one hundred years later a Dutchman named Abel Tasman sailed around Australia and discovered a large island, now named Tasmania after him. Tasman reached New Zealand. In 1642, Captain Tasman landed in the Tonga Islands because he needed food and water. He received a friendly welcome from the people.

However, most of the South Pacific was not really explored until after the middle of the eighteenth century. Captain James Cook was an Englishman who explored the Pacific from Alaska to New Zealand. In 1768, Captain Cook took a party of scientists to Tahiti to observe the planet Venus as it passed unusually close to the earth. Tahiti and other islands in French Polynesia had been seen and briefly explored by another English captain, named Samuel Wallis, in 1767, and by the Frenchman, Captain Louis de Bougainville, in 1768.

Cook visited the South Pacific again between 1771 and

Breadfruit trees grow on all the islands.

1774. He charted islands, located reefs, and added greatly to knowledge of the area.

The story of the next explorer has been made famous in a book and a motion picture. In 1788, a young British Naval Lieutenant named William Bligh was sent to the South Pacific on an unusual mission. He was to fill his ship, the *Bounty,* with breadfruit seedlings which were then to be taken to the British-held islands of the Caribbean.

Tahiti was chosen because the Polynesians there were generally friendly. The *Bounty* was loaded with breadfruit seedlings, and in April 1789, began her long voyage to the Caribbean. The ship made a stop in the Tonga Islands to take on fuel and water. Two days later the crew of the *Bounty* mutinied.

Lieutenant William Bligh and eighteen other loyal men were put into a twenty-three-foot boat, with a little water and bread, and set adrift. The small boat could not return to Tahiti or other friendly islands, because the wind was blowing in the other direction. Bligh decided to set a course for an island in the Dutch East Indies, 3,600 miles away.

Even though Bligh and his men were starved and sick and sometimes chased by unfriendly war canoes, they did a remarkable job of charting islands and reefs and channels. In his journal Bligh describes some of his adventures. On May 7, 1789, he wrote, "This day I discovered ten other islands, and at noon was chased by two large canoes . . ."

On June 14, 1789, the small boat reached Timor in the Dutch East Indies. Bligh had safely sailed 3,600 miles through islands many of which had never before been seen by Europeans.

In 1792, Bligh, now a captain, visited Tahiti again. This time he was able to finish his job. The breadfruit seedlings which he took to the West Indies at that time have now spread to every Caribbean island. This fruit, which is cooked before eating, has become one of the most important foods of the Caribbean.*

The mutineers sailed the *Bounty* back to Tahiti. Some of

* See *Let's Visit the West Indies* (John Day Company, N.Y.).

the men landed there, while others sailed on to Pitcairn Island, where they lived in secret for many years.

During the next fifty years there were other explorers, British, French, German, Russian and also American. In 1839 and 1840, an American naval exploring mission, commanded by Commodore Charles Wilkes, visited Samoa and established American claims to those islands. Wilkes sailed through the Fiji Islands, and his charts were the first accurate charts of this part of the South Pacific.

In 1797, a British ship named the *Duff* arrived in the South Pacific. The *Duff* carried people who were to have a great effect on the lives of the island people. The ship belonged to the London Missionary Society and carried missionaries who were to begin work in Tahiti, the Fiji and Tonga islands.

There were also other Europeans who began to settle in the Pacific Islands, at first by accident. In 1800, 1803 or 1806 (we are not sure of the year) the schooner *Argo* was wrecked on one of the many coral reefs in the Fiji Islands. Most of the crew members were killed and eaten. A few men were allowed to live, almost as slaves of the Fijian chiefs.

There were other wrecks, and often crew members were able to persuade the islanders not to eat them. From time to time adventurers landed and established homes on islands. Many of these early white men were called *beachcombers*. There were Englishmen, Australians and Americans. Some were criminals, and many were dishonest.

We might say that for many years there was a contest in the South Pacific between the missionaries and the beach-combers. The missionaries were trying to end the bloodshed, the wars between different island tribes, the eating of human beings. There were friendly peoples; the Tonga Islands were named Friendly Islands by Captain Cook, who was impressed by the peaceful people. But on other islands, especially the Fiji group, cannibalism and tribal wars were common. The beachcombers made conditions worse by bringing in guns and whisky. We will learn more about European settlement as we read about the different island groups.

Let's begin with a visit to the Fiji Islands, a British Crown Colony with a larger area and population than any of the other South Pacific Island groups.

THE FIJI ISLANDS

Once known as the Cannibal Islands, the Fiji group has the largest area and population of the islands we will visit in this book. The daily newspaper published in the Fiji Islands, *The Fiji Times,* brags that it is the first paper to reach the newsstands each day anywhere in the world. And the Fijians and their neighbors living in the Tonga Islands say that they are the first people to get up and greet the sun every day.

The *International Date Line* is an imaginary line at which the date must be advanced one day when one is traveling west and put back one day when one is traveling east. This line runs north and south through the Pacific from the Bering Straits to Antarctica, and passes just to the east of the Fiji Islands. For this reason it is already Monday morning in Fiji when it is still Sunday a few hundred miles to the east.

The Fiji Islands have a more interesting history than that of any other Pacific Islands. We will learn how the United States played a part in this history. We will also read about people on one island who can call sea turtles by chanting a song. On another island there are men who can walk barefooted across red-hot coals and rocks, without burning their feet. The *Firewalkers* and *Turtlecallers* are but two of the interesting groups of people to be learned about in the Fiji Islands.

About Geography and Weather

Let's locate the Fiji island group on the map. The islands lie west of the international date line and about 1,200 miles south of the equator. From Suva, the capital, it is 3,183 miles to Honolulu, 1,300 miles to Auckland, New Zealand, and 2,800 miles to Sydney, Australia.

There are 320 islands in the Fiji group, of which 106 are inhabited. The total land area is 7,022 square miles, somewhat smaller than the size of New Jersey. The total population is about 450,000. Over half the total area is found on

Viti Levu. Other large islands are named Vanau Levu, Taveuni and Kadavu.

The larger islands of the Fiji group are all high islands. We have learned that this means that they were formed by volcanic action. However, unlike Tahiti and other large islands in French Polynesia, the Fiji Islands are *old*. The mountains are, for the most part, rounded and not as high.

We have already read about the effect of the trade winds on the climate and rainfall of Pacific Islands. On this and the next page there are pictures of Viti Levu which show this effect clearly. This island lies in an east-west direction.

This picture shows the dry side of Viti Levu.

AUTHOR

The first picture was made on the northern side of the island; the other picture on the southeast coast.

The north and northwest part of Viti Levu have a rainfall of 50 to 60 inches a year. The mountains are covered with grass and a few trees. The south and southeastern coasts are very wet. Rainfall averages over 120 inches, and sometimes there are over 200 inches of rain. The mountains are covered with thick, tropical jungles. The trade winds blow from the southeast, and when these winds strike the mountainous south coast of Viti Levu, the moisture falls in the form of heavy rains.

All the islands lie within the Tropical zone, and the

There are jungles on the wet side.

AUTHOR

In the Fiji Islands there are broad valleys.

weather is warm. There is a hot, rainy season from December through February. Since the Fiji Islands are south of the equator, the rainy season is Fiji's summertime. During this period the temperature may be as high as 90 degrees. In July — or midwinter — the days are pleasantly warm, and nights may be quite cool.

Because of its size, Viti Levu is different from any of the other larger South Pacific Islands. There are large rivers; the mountains, though rising to over 4,000 feet, are not too rugged, and therefore the island has a good network of

39

highways. The only railroad in the South Pacific is located on this island, and this railroad is the only one in the world providing *free* passenger service.

There are big villages in the interior of Viti Levu and the other large islands of the Fiji group. The several large rivers and the broad valleys have made transportation easy. The new and rugged high islands of the South Pacific have almost no population, except along the seacoast. The mountains are too rough for roads, except along the shoreline.

European Settlement

We have already read that the first Europeans arrived in Fiji by accident in 1800, when a ship was wrecked on one of the many coral reefs. Some of the crew members were killed and eaten. A few men were allowed to live. There were other wrecks during the next few years. Although many of the sailors were killed, a few managed to persuade the Fijians to spare them.

Two discoveries soon helped to bring many foreign ships to the Fiji Islands. Fragrant-smelling sandalwood was found growing on several islands. This wood was in great demand among the Chinese. Between 1805 and 1840, scores of sailing vessels came to Fiji for cargoes of sandalwood.

At about the time sandalwood was becoming scarce another thriving business started. Again it was the Chinese who supplied the market. The Chinese are very fond of *sea slugs,* usually called by the French name, *bêche-de-mer.* There are many sea slugs in the warm waters around the Fiji Islands. The slugs were gathered from the sea, cooked, then dried for shipment to Manila or China ports.

There were many ships, including American vessels, engaged in the sandalwood and *bêche-de-mer* trade. In order to get the cooperation of the Fijian chiefs, the traders often provided the Fijians with whisky and guns. Sometimes, in exchange for the right to collect sea slugs or sandalwood, a trader would agree to help one chief wage war against rival chiefs.

The Fiji Islands became inhabited by the white men called beachcombers. The wars between chiefs became bloodier than ever. Before the coming of Europeans, the Fijians had fought with clubs and spears. Now that guns were available it was possible to kill more rivals and to have bigger feasts of human bodies. The white beachcombers did not care what the Fijians did as long as they were able to make money. As we have said, the missionaries tried to change the Fijian way of life.

However, not all Europeans were beachcombers. In addition to the missionaries, there were Australians, New Zealanders and a few Americans who opened trading posts or began to farm and ranch.

The missionaries found no written language when they arrived. One of their earliest tasks was to create an alphabet so that the Bible could be translated into the Fijian language.

A waterfall on Viti Levu's wet side

ROB WRIGHT

There are over forty different *dialects* spoken in the Fiji Islands. However, these dialects are somewhat similar. The missionaries soon developed a 24-letter alphabet. In 1838, the first printing press was brought to the islands. Soon there were many classes learning the alphabet.

Since we will learn the names of some Fijians and some places in the islands, let's learn how to pronounce Fijian letters and words. The emphasis is almost always placed on the next to the last syllable of each word. And we must learn that although using the letters of our alphabet, this language uses quite different pronunciation for several of the letters.

B is pronounced MB, as in *number*
C is pronounced TH, as in *that*
D is pronounced ND, as in *end*
G is pronounced NG, as in *sing*
Q is pronounced NG, as in *finger*

Let's see how words are pronounced. The most famous Fijian king was named *Cakobau* (pronounced Tha-ko-mbau). The island of Beqa, famous for its firewalkers, is pronounced Mbengga. The big airport on the island of Viti Levu is pronounced Nandi but is correctly spelled Nadi.

There are a number of English words in the Fijian language. One interesting word is *kali,* the word for dog. Until the coming of Europeans, there were no dogs in the islands. It is thought that some early settler had a collie dog. Ever since that time all dogs have been called kali.

In another section we will learn that three different languages are used in the Fiji Islands. But now let's read about how an American celebration changed the history of the islands.

John Brown Williams and the 4th of July

There were good and bad Americans among the beachcombers and settlers. In 1840, John Brown Williams of Salem, Massachusetts, arrived and started business as a trader. On July 4, 1849, Williams and some American friends were celebrating by shooting off firecrackers. One of the men decided to fire an old cannon. The cannon misfired, setting Williams' house on fire.

John Brown Williams was not popular among the Fijians. When the house was set on fire, local villagers took advantage of the confusion to steal most of the trader's belongings. Williams claimed that his losses amounted to $5,000.38. Each time an American warship visited Fiji, Williams asked in vain for the commander's help in collecting his claim.

In 1853, Williams' house and store were broken into; in 1855, his house was burned again. The original claim against the Fijians increased to $30,000 and finally to $42,531. A United States Navy ship arrived in Fiji waters in 1855, and this time Williams persuaded the ship's officer to help him.

King Cakobau was invited aboard the warship. Once on the ship, the king was presented a document to sign. The document stated that he promised to pay the $42,531 within two years. King Cakobau was forced to sign. He was told that unless he did so, he would be made a prisoner and taken to America.

It is doubtful if the value of Williams' belongings amounted to more than a few thousand dollars. The way in which the Fijian king was forced to sign the agreement certainly was unfair. And the pressure and threats against him in the years that followed were also unfair. But the events did help to shape the history of the islands.

King Cakobau knew that he could never raise such a

large sum of money. He offered to *give* his country to England, provided the English Government would pay the $42,531! But the Government of Great Britain did not want the responsibility of governing a group of islands where men still ate one another, and the first offer was refused.

By this time there were several thousand white settlers in the islands. Although King Cakobau claimed to rule all the islands, he actually had little power. Conditions were unsettled; there was war between tribes and attacks on the settlers. For many years there was war or threat of war between Fiji and nearby Tonga.

When the British Government refused to accept the islands, the white settlers and some leading Fijian chiefs wrote a petition to the President of the United States, offering to cede the islands to our Government. The King was agreeable to this idea because if the United States owned Fiji, the $42,531 debt might be forgotten. But the President did not answer the petition.

John Brown Williams' troubles started the white settlers and the growing number of Christian chiefs to thinking about the future of the Fiji Islands. The American Civil War brought many changes in the Fiji Islands. Eventually King Cakobau's offer was accepted.

Cotton, Slavery and Cession

The American Civil War stopped shipment of cotton

from the Southern states to England. The blockade of Southern ports by the Union Navy caused a world-wide shortage of cotton. Farmers in other parts of the world immediately began to raise cotton so that they could take advantage of the shortage.

Hundreds of Australian, New Zealand and English settlers came into the Fiji Islands. They sometimes bought and sometimes stole land from the people. By 1862, there were thousands of acres of cotton under cultivation.

It is strange that the American Civil War, fought to free slaves, created slavery in the Pacific Islands. The Fijians were unwilling to work on plantations, so the planters solved this problem by getting workers from other island groups all over the South Pacific.

Labor ships visited islands 1,000 and more miles from Fiji. Sometimes a chief was bribed to provide workers. The planters on Fiji paid for the workers secured; the crew on the labor ships were paid "head" money, or a certain amount for each laborer brought to Fiji.

The laborers were supposed to work for three years with reasonably good pay and a promise of free transportation back to their home islands. In reality, the agreements were rarely honored. As the demand for workers increased, hundreds of people were kidnapped. Often local chiefs traded men and women for guns and whisky.

The men and ships engaged in the labor traffic were called *blackbirders*. The way in which they operated and the treatment of workers by the Fiji planters became a disgrace. Authorities in Australia and in England demanded that blackbirding be stopped. In 1872, the British Government passed a kidnapping act known as the Polynesian Islanders Protection Act. Any British citizen found in the business could be arrested and his ships confiscated.

Meanwhile the Civil War had kept American naval ships too busy to visit the Fiji Islands. Everyone seemed to have forgotten the United States' claim against King Cakobau. However, in 1867, American warships began to visit the South Pacific again. John Brown Williams' claim and others had not been forgotten after all. King Cakobau was told that the warships would bombard his islands unless he agreed to make a first payment within a year.

The king's government was poor. He had little control over the tribes living inland or on outlying islands. Conditions were so unsettled that he could not collect taxes. For several years the white settlers and the king had tried to govern the islands in a democratic and orderly way. A constitution was drafted, and the king had a cabinet including several Europeans.

The Fiji Government had little money and could not even protect its citizens. In 1873, a white planter, his family and eighteen workers were massacred by hill tribesmen. From time to time there were other killings and continued wars between tribes.

The blackbirders, the killing of white settlers, wars between rival chiefs and the claim against King Cakobau started by John Brown Williams — all these combined to cause the British Government finally to accept the king's offer of cession.

On October 10, 1874, the king signed an agreement giving the Fiji Islands to Great Britain. The king's flag was lowered; the British flag raised. As a final part of the ceremony, King Cakobau handed over his war club to be sent to Queen Victoria. The Fiji Islands became a British Crown Colony. Cannibalism and war between tribes ended.

About the People

What do the people of Fiji look like? They are dark-skinned, as we can see in the pictures. We have already learned that they are Melanesians and probably came from Africa long ago. However, if you lived in the Fiji Islands, you might or might not be a Fijian.

On this page there is a picture of a school ground. The sign saying NO THOROUGHFARE is written in three languages.

The Fijian girl is on the right.

English is at the top. Below the English words are the same words in Fijian.

Can you guess what the third language could be? The strange-looking letters are *Hindi,* the most important of the many languages spoken in India. The children you see in the picture are Indian children, and the school is an Indian school. There are more Indians living in the Fiji Islands than there are Fijians!

If you were to visit the Fiji Islands, you might at first have trouble telling a Fijian from an Indian. Although belonging to the white branch of the human family, many Indians are dark-skinned.

On this page there is a picture of an Indian girl and a

Fijian girl. The children are much alike, are they not? The main difference to a newcomer is the hair. The word *frizzly* is often used to describe the hair of Fijians. Indians, on the other hand, have straight, black hair.

Why are there so many Indians in the Fiji Islands? We have already read about the blackbirders and the slave laborers brought to Fiji from other islands throughout the Pacific. Some of the laborers stayed on; many others were sent back to their homes when blackbirding was made unlawful. The problem of finding enough farm and plantation workers was still not solved. And so in 1877, the Fiji Islands' government sent a representative to India to secure a small but regular number of Indian workers each year.

The Indians were needed as farm workers and also as domestic servants. During this period Indians were also immigrants to other British territories, especially to Trinidad, in the West Indies.

Indian workers could return to India when their terms of service were finished. But few Indians wanted to return to a homeland where there was so often not enough to eat. Instead, the men sent back to India for their families. When Indian boys were old enough to marry, they went back to India to find wives.

In addition to many people from India, there are also Indian animals in Fiji. The only common animal, the two most common birds, and an abundant fruit come from India. The *mongoose* is the animal. Mongooses were brought

Church and school in the Fiji Islands

from India to destroy the snakes and rats that came to the islands from ships. The small mongooses have done their job well; there are very few snakes. Unfortunately, mongooses also like chickens and have become a problem to farmers. And they have killed off many kinds of ground-nesting birds, including the wild chickens that were once found on Viti Levu.

51

The *mynah* bird and the *bulbul* are also natives of India. Mynahs can sometimes be taught to talk, or at least to make sounds like words. It is said that the mynahs were also brought to Fiji to help destroy snakes. The birds often make a big fuss if they see a snake. No one seems to know why the bulbul was brought to the South Pacific. About the size of a towhee, or sparrow, this little bird is pretty but very noisy.

Finally, the delicious *mango* came from India and is an important fruit. The mango is an oblong, yellow-red fruit with a thick rind and juicy pulp.

There are now about 195,000 Indians in the Fiji Islands, approximately 175,000 Fijians and 9,000 Europeans. Almost 50 percent of the population is Indian! In addition, there are about 1,000 people from other South Pacific Islands and almost 5,000 Chinese.

We have read about the beginning of missionary work in the Fiji Islands. As a result of this work, all Fijians are Christians. There are many more Catholics than Protestants. And among the Protestants there are more members of the Methodist Church than of any other denomination.

Among the Indians there are many *Hindus,* some *Mohammedans,* and a few *Sikhs.** These are the principal religions of India, and there are Mohammedan mosques and Hindu and Sikh temples in the Fiji Islands. There are also a few Buddhists among the 5,000 Chinese.

* See *Let's Visit India* and *Let's Visit Pakistan* by the same author (John Day Company, New York).

The Indians work on sugar plantations, on other large farms, and in town and city stores. The Chinese are almost always store owners. Fijians are more often small farmers, fishermen, sometimes workers in big stores.

At the time the Europeans began settlement of the islands, the Fijians often did not cut their hair. It was allowed to grow in a big circle, as much as three feet around. When I was visiting Suva, the capital of Fiji, I took a picture of a hotel doorman. His head of hair is still quite large. The early settlers called these Fijian men the "big heads." There are only a few big heads in Fiji now.

AUTHOR

Indian women wear saris.

Many Indians and Fijians wear western-style clothes like those worn by the people in our country. However, Indian women usually wear the Indian *sari* (pronounced SAH-ree). The sari is a long wrap-around skirt, in pretty colors. It is worn with a blouse. A few Indian men wear the *dhoti* (pronounced DOE-tee). This is a long, wide piece of cloth wrapped around the waist and passed between the legs.

Fijian women usually wear long skirts and blouses. And even the men wear skirts. The Fijian men's skirt is called a *sulu* (pronounced SOO-loo). Sometimes the hem of the sulu is cut in fancy scallops.

All the Fijian traffic policemen wear white sulus, red-and-black belts, dark blue shirts and white gloves. Sometimes American visitors cause traffic jams because they stop to take pictures of the colorful policemen.

A Fijian Village

Fijians who live in the towns and cities have houses much like those of other people. But in the countryside, in the mountain valleys and on the smaller islands, the Fijian village is much like it was when the Europeans arrived. On this and the next page there are pictures of Fijian villages.

The Fijian thatched hut is called a *bure* (pronounced BOOR-eh). Sometimes the bure is circular in shape, sometimes it is built like a rectangle. The sides are made of split

Fijian villages are often built on river banks.

A Fijian village scene

bamboo. Often the floor is hard-packed earth, or if a family has enough money, there may be a wood floor. Since bures are made entirely of material found nearby in the jungles, they cost very little. No glass windows are needed, as it never gets cold.

The family may sleep on the floor, or sometimes the father and mother have a bed and the children sleep on the floor. Except among wealthy people, there is very little furniture. The family sits on the floor, and eats from mats placed on the floor.

We have read about the Fiji chiefs who used to rule the islands. King Cakobau was a chief who ruled more than one district. There were village chiefs and district chiefs, and these men had complete authority over all their subjects. A chief could take away a man's house; could order him killed and eaten.

When Great Britain accepted the islands from King Cakobau, it was agreed that Fijian chiefs would retain considerable authority. Each district and village still has a chief whose house usually is the largest and best built in a village. Many Fijians hold a chief in such respect that they bow low before him, or even lie flat on the ground.

Fijian villages are always located near water. There are

A Fijian bure

ROB WRIGHT

Going to town in a "put-put"

large villages along the coast and in the big river valleys. Fijians love the water and are expert swimmers and boatmen. In the old days they built double-decker war canoes over 100 feet long.

Boats are still important as a means of transportation and for fishing. However, except in the outlying islands, there are few outrigger canoes used now. Outrigger canoes have a device built out on one side to keep them from turning upside down in the water. Fijians like to own a motorboat or an outboard motor which they call a "put-put." Here is a picture of Fijians traveling to town in a put-put.

The larger Fijian villages are becoming quite modern. There may be electricity and running water in a village. Corrugated tin roofs are often used now instead of thatch. Yet in many ways Fijian life has not changed. Important news is still announced by a "town crier," just as it was many years ago. People farm in the same primitive way and like the same foods.

On the next page there is a picture showing two of the most important food crops. The plant with the large leaves is *taro*. The taro root is big and starchy and is cooked. The tall plants with narrow fingerlike leaves are tapioca bushes. The root of the tapioca is also large and rich in starch. Tapioca, taro and yams (sweet potatoes) are important foods.

Breadfruit and bananas grow throughout the islands. Both these fruits are usually cooked. With the cooked fruit or vegetable, the family will often have fish. The seas around the islands are rich in fish and other sea food.

For a special feast occasion, Fijians like roast suckling pig. Whether it is a feast or an every-day meal, people eat with their fingers.

Farms and Farming

Sugar cane is by far the most important crop. In most other sugar-cane-growing countries, the cane is grown on large plantations. In Fiji, the cane is grown by farmers on their small farms, and sold to the big sugar mills.

When the Europeans arrived, sugar cane was found growing wild. The first large sugar mill was established in 1882. There are now four large mills, all operated by the big Colonial Sugar Refining Company.

We have read that the only free railroad in the world operates in Viti Levu Island. The railroad is a narrow-gauge one, with tiny engines and cars. It was built to carry sugar cane from the fields to the mills. The sugar company agreed to pay rent to all Fijians through whose land the railroad passed. This proved to be very complicated, as there were so many little payments to be made. The company finally decided to make an agreement with the chiefs,

The big-leaved plant is taro. The plant with leaves like fingers is tapioca.

AUTHOR

This is the free train.

allowing all Fijians to ride free on the train, if the Fijians would forget about the rent. And so it is that even though there are highways with much faster travel by bus, Fijians like their free train. It is always crowded all along the 120 miles of its run.

Sugar cane grows only on the dry side of Viti Levu. The cane grows from cuttings planted in the fields. When it is ready to harvest, the farmers cut the stalks off at the ground, with sharp knives. The cane may be carried to the mills on the company railroad, by truck, even by oxcart. During

Sugar cane going to market

harvesttime, portable railway tracks are laid down right into the fields. The sugar-filled stalks are loaded on little cars and taken to either the main railway line or to a highway. When all the cane in one field has been cut, the workers pick up the tracks and lay them down in another field.

Next in importance to sugar cane is *copra*. The white meat of the coconut is rich in oil, and when dried is called copra. This oil is used in cooking, in making margarine and soap.

There are many coconut palms on Viti Levu and all the

other islands. Little schooners make regular trips to the smaller islands, to pick up the dried copra and take it to the pressing mill or to Suva for shipment.

Coconuts are not picked. The owners wait until the coconuts drop to the ground. It is interesting to know that Fijians, Tahitians and other island people of the South Pacific, do not build their houses directly under coconut palms. Paths do not run under trees, but rather between the palms. A big coconut dropping from 40 or 50 feet can be very dangerous!

In recent years a big beetle known as the *rhinoceros beetle* has killed many coconut palms. The government of Fiji sends men all through the islands, trying to find and destroy the beetles and their young, called larvae (pronounced LAHR-vee).

Copra is not as important a product now as it was a few years ago. *Synthetic* oils have been invented and are used in making soap and margarine. However, people on the outlying islands still depend on copra, to trade for clothing and other supplies.

Sugar cane is the important crop of the dry side of Viti Levu. On the wet side, bananas are the main crop. Around every village there are also fields of tapioca and taro.

Church and School

If you were to take a trip on any Sunday, you would not

see farmwork going on, and almost all stores would be closed. The Fijians are now all Christians. As we learned, because the first missionaries were Methodists, there are more members of this denomination than any other. But there are also numerous Catholics, Seventh-Day Adventists and Mormons.

Of whatever denomination, the Fijian family dresses up and goes to church on Sunday. Fijians love to sing and have fine voices. They like all kinds of music. It is said that for many years the Salvation Army was not allowed to operate in the islands. The Salvation Army often uses a small band to attract people. It was feared that the music-

Everybody goes to church on Sunday.

ROB WRIGHT

loving Fijians would hear the bands and would leave the other churches, which had no band music.

Almost all Fijian boys and girls have Biblical names. This also is true of other islands in the South Pacific. The Fijians sometimes like unusual Biblical names like *Obadiah* or *Uriah*.

The Christian denominations, Catholic and Protestant, all operate schools. This is important, because there is no free education in Fiji. Education is not compulsory. This means that boys and girls are not required by the law of the land to go to school.

The cost of going to elementary school may be as high as $30 a year. This would not be much money in our country, but for many Fijian and Indian families it is a small fortune. The cost of going to high school is even greater.

Even so, there are hundreds of schools. As we have said, the churches often operate schools. There are government schools, Indian schools and Fijian village schools. All elementary school children wear uniforms.

In the elementary schools, children of different races go to different schools. Fijian children go to their own village schools; Indian boys and girls attend their Hindu or Moslem schools; and the children of the Europeans have their schools. In high school the races are mixed.

Although the state law does not require children to go to school, the Fijian tribal laws require as much education as possible. In spite of the cost, most families will manage to get their children into school for a few years. Among Fijians, education is considered so important that children living on small islands will often travel several miles by canoe each day to reach a school on another island.

Almost all teaching is in English. For this reason, most boys and girls read and speak some English. It is only among the old people, both Fijian and Indian, that we find people unable to speak or understand English.

Did you know that there are many differences in the way Americans and English speak the English language? In Fiji, boys and girls learn the English way of saying things. Here are a few examples: gasoline is called petrol; the hood of a car is called the bonnet; and trucks are called lorries.

Fun and Games

During World War II many American soldiers were stationed in the Fiji Islands. The Americans played baseball and tried to teach the Fijians to play our national game. However, everyone — Fijian, Indian and European — preferred the sports popular in England.

Soccer, Rugby and cricket are the most popular sports in the Fijis today. Soccer and Rugby are both called "football," but are different from our game of football. In playing soccer, a round ball is used, and the object of the game is to kick the ball between the goal posts. However, any part of the body, except the hands, may be used. A good soccer player knows how to use his head! Often a good player will use his head or chest to bounce the ball to another player on his side.

Rugby is a rougher game than soccer. The ball is shaped somewhat like our football. The players try to get the ball across the goal line and between the goal posts. However, unlike soccer, the ball may be carried and passed, as well as kicked. The player who has the ball may be tackled.

In Rugby, when the ball goes out of bounds, it is put back into play by rolling or tossing it among all the players, who are crowded together as in a huddle. With over twenty players trying to get at the ball with their hands and feet, Rugby can be a rough game.

On this page there is a picture of Fijian, Indian, European and Chinese boys, all playing together. Indian boys

French, Tahitian and Chinese boys play together.

AUTHOR

AUTHOR

Soccer and Rugby field in Suva

like soccer best, while Fijian boys enjoy the much rougher Rugby.

Another English game that is played in Fiji is called *bowls*. This game is somewhat like our bowling. The main difference is that it is played outdoors and on the grass. First, a little white ball is rolled from one end of the bowling field to the other. Then the object is to see how close each player can bowl his ball to the little white ball.

The ball used is smaller than our bowling ball. It is

The Welcoming ceremony

weighted on one side, so that it will roll in a crazy way. A good bowls player can make the ball curve so that it will miss other balls and come close to the white ball.

Bowls players come to Fiji from Australia and New Zealand, to play against Fiji teams. The annual bowls tournament is an important sporting event.

Living as they do, close to the ocean, Fijian children are good swimmers. Everybody learns to swim, and all boys and girls enjoy the water, which is never too cold for swimming.

Interesting Legends and Customs

On this page is a picture of Fijians welcoming a visitor to their village. The visiting guests are seated in chairs, and the villagers are seated on the ground. One Fijian man is wearing a black sula and white shirt, and is standing with a small bowl in his hands.

The people in the picture are welcoming their guests with what is called the *yanquona* or *kava* ceremony. Kava is a drink always used to welcome visitors, and there is always a ceremony when this drink is served. Kava is made from the roots of a small bush. It is dirty white in color. Europeans often say that kava looks like dishwater and tastes like dishwater.

In the kava ceremony a large wooden bowl is used to make the drink by mashing the roots and mixing with water. All the village elders sit near the bowl, facing the guests of honor. When the kava is ready, one of the elders presents it to the guests of honor in a smaller bowl. Even though kava does not taste good if you are not used to it, it is important for guests to drink it down to the last drop. Otherwise the feelings of the village people would be hurt. The kava ceremony is still followed everywhere in the Fiji Islands.

Fijians like to sing and dance. Dances are called *mekes,* and they tell some ancient legend or story. There are spear dances which tell the story of a long-ago battle. There are men's mekes and women's mekes. Some of these are performed sitting, while others are performed standing. A chorus sits nearby and claps and chants the story that is being acted out by the dancers. For special occasions men and women perform the mekes dressed in the tribal costumes of long ago. In mekes which tell the story of battles, the men paint their faces and cover their hair with a yellow dye.

Some Fijian customs are very unusual and cannot be explained by science. One of the mysterious customs is that of firewalking. This is a strange art which can only be practiced by the men of the Sawau tribe of Bequa (pronounced Mben-ga) Island. Firewalking is based on a Sawau legend and takes place now only on special occasions.

A women's meke

ROB WRIGHT

Firewalkers

On this page there is a picture showing part of this ceremony. In the center of the picture is a pit filled with round
stones. A big fire is built over the stones, and after several
hours the stones become red hot. At a signal from a village
elder, a group of village youths rush from hiding and each
one walks barefooted across the red-hot stones. Even though
the stones are so hot that a bit of dried grass thrown into the
pit will burst into flames, the firewalkers are not burned!

Around each firewalker's ankle there is a band of dried
fern leaves. While anything else — even a piece of cloth

72

thrown into the pit — will burst into flame, the dried fern bands do not catch on fire. The feet of the firewalkers have often been carefully examined after the ceremony. There are no signs of burns! No one knows how the firewalkers perform this ceremony, and only the members of one tribe are able to do it.

The women of Namuana Villaga of the island of Kadavu (pronounced Kah-NDAH-voo) have a custom that also is difficult to explain. The custom is based on a Fijian legend about two women of the village who were captured by a war canoe from another village. Suddenly there was a great storm and the canoe was about to be swamped in the waves. The men in the canoe then noticed that the two captured women had changed into big sea turtles. Quickly the turtles were thrown into the sea, and the storm ended as suddenly as it began.

Supposedly it is the descendants of these two women who now have the power of calling turtles. Several times each year, all the women of the village climb to the side of a hill overlooking the sea. They begin to chant a strange-sounding song. As the women sing, great sea turtles begin to rise to the surface of the ocean. Often there may be scores of sea turtles on the surface of the water, listening to the song. As soon as the women stop singing the turtles disappear.

If any person from the nearby village of Nebukelevu (pronounced Neh-mboo-ke-LE-voo) is present at the ceremony, the turtles will not rise to the surface. It was the war canoe from this village that — according to the legend — captured the two Namuana women long, long ago!

The stories of the firewalkers and the turtlecallers are not fairy stories. The ceremonies actually take place and can be watched by people who have the time to visit the islands of Bequa and Kadavu.

The Cities of Fiji

Suva, the capital of the colony of Fiji, is the largest city in the South Pacific Islands. Its population of 40,000 includes many Indians, Fijians, Europeans, Chinese and people from almost every other island group in the South Pacific.

The city is built on a deep lagoon, which makes it an excellent port. Big steamers are able to enter the lagoon through a break in the barrier reef. American ships from San Francisco visit Suva regularly on the way to and from New Zealand and Australia.

Being on the wet side of Viti Levu, Suva is a city of many gardens. The tropical jungle comes to the edge of the city. There is an airport nearby with service to Nadi, the international airport on the other end of Viti Levu. Two large highways meet at Suva. One highway is called the King's Road, and it follows the northeast coast to Lautoka, the second city in size. The Queen's Road is the other highway, and it follows the south-west coast to Lautoka. The distance all around the island on these two highways is 326 miles.

Government House is located in the capital city of Suva. Now let's read about the government of the islands.

The Government of Fiji

We have learned that Fiji is a British Crown Colony. The Queen of England is represented by a governor. A legislative council assists the governor. One half of this council is elected, and one half is appointed by the governor. This means that there is some self-government in the islands. However, the governor really does have the final say on all matters, because he has a veto power over the actions of the legislative council, and his veto cannot be overruled.

The elected members of the council are equally divided among Fijians, Indians and Europeans. Since there are over 200,000 Indians and almost 175,000 Fijians, compared to 10,000 Europeans, this means that the European minority has as much voice as either of the other racial groups.

Some Fijian leaders and most of the Indian leaders do not like this system. They would like to see a government in which each race is represented according to its population. However, this is not likely to occur. The Indians are not popular with either Europeans or Fijians. As more and more Fijians become educated they feel they should have more rights, since the islands are really their islands.

But we should not think that there is trouble between

races. There is no social segregation. This means that members of all races may eat together, go to the same hotels and motion-picture theatres. As we have said, Fijian children go to Fijian schools, and Indian children go to their own schools, but this is a matter of choice and not because of segregation laws.

Great Britain has given independence to many of its colonies since the end of World War II. In other colonies the people have been given more self-government. It is unlikely that the Fiji Islands will become an independent country in the near future. Although some Indians talk about independence, most Fijians do not want to be independent. They realize that the islands need the help and protection of Great Britain. Fijians would like to have a greater voice in the government, but most of the people are happy to be citizens of a British colony.

As we end our visit to the Fiji Islands we should learn about other islands of the South Pacific that are also under the authority of the British Government.

The Tonga Islands and Pitcairn Island

The Tonga or Friendly Islands lie about 200 miles southeast of the eastern group of the Fiji Islands. There are more than 150 islands, but the land area is only 269 square miles. The total population is about 70,000.

The Kingdom of Tonga is more or less independent, but is under the protection of Great Britain.

Most of the Tonga Islands are low, covered with palm

trees, and surrounded by coral reefs. In the north there are a few high islands. Unlike the Fijians, the Tongans are Polynesians. For many years the Tongans waged war against the Fijians. The two island groups have been closely related, and for this reason there are many part-Polynesian people in the eastern islands of the Fiji group.

The Tongans became Christian in the early nineenth century, and the first premier of the kingdom was a Methodist minister. The Tongans sent missionaries to Fiji in 1838. It is said that King George of Tonga persuaded King Cakobau of Fiji to become a Christian.

The Kingdom of Tonga is now ruled by a queen whose name is Salote. There is a legislative assembly of 22 members, made up of 7 nobles, 7 representatives elected by the people, and 7 members of the cabinet and the speaker, who are appointed by the queen. The islands have a progressive government, with free medical attention and compulsory education.

Pitcairn Island is famous because mutineers from the *Bounty* landed there in 1790 and lived in secrecy for nearly twenty years before being discovered. The island is administered from Fiji, even though it is 2,000 miles to the east of Suva. Pitcairn is a high island of only 2 square miles and has only 160 inhabitants.

FRENCH POLYNESIA

Tahiti is probably the best known of the South Pacific

Islands. Several authors have lived there and written about the island. We have read that Robert Louis Stevenson was one of these.

However, Tahiti has only one-tenth of the population of the Fiji Islands. It is but one of 130 islands governed by France and making up the territory of French Polynesia.

The islands of French Polynesia are scattered over an area of the Pacific as large as all of Europe, with the exception of Russia. But the total land area of the 130 islands is only about 2,500 square miles, or less than the area of Rhode Island. The total population of French Polynesia is about 80,000. Over half the people live on the island of Tahiti. Papeete, on Tahiti, is the capital city.

We will first learn the names and locations of the different groups that make up French Polynesia.

Tahiti is the largest of the Society Islands, named by Captain Cook in honor of the Royal Geographical Society of England. It is located in the South Pacific, 3,700 miles from Los Angeles and almost directly south of the Hawaiian Islands. The distance to Australia is 3,300 miles, so the island is nearly halfway between our continent and Australia.

The Society Islands are divided into two groups, the Windward and the Leeward islands. Tahiti and Moorea are the largest of the Windward Islands. Bora Bora, Raiatea and Tahaa are the largest of the Leeward group and are from 90 to 135 miles from Tahiti. Three-fourths of the population of all French Polynesia lives in the Society Islands, with almost half the people living on Tahiti.

All of the Society Islands, with the exception of little off-shore atolls, are new high islands. Mount Orohena on Tahiti is 7,350 feet high and is the highest mountain in the South Pacific. We have learned that new volcanic islands are mountainous and that the mountains are often high and jagged in appearance.

The Marquesas Islands are almost 900 miles northeast of Tahiti. The six main islands of this group are all high islands. The total population is only 5,000. There is no regular steamship service to the Marquesas Islands, and planes call only twice a month. Very few outsiders have ever seen these lovely islands.

The Tuamotu Archipelago is a long chain of 82 low islands or atolls, of which 23 are inhabited. These islands, being closer to Tahiti, have weekly seaplane service and are famous for their beautiful lagoons, fishing, and mother-of-pearl products.

The Gambier Islands lie to the south of the Tuamotus and are high islands enclosed in a lagoon which is surrounded by a chain of small atolls. The Tuamotu and the Gambier islands are administered together and have a total population of about 9,000. The four high Austral Islands, with a population of 4,000, are 300 miles south of Tahiti.

The People of French Polynesia

Among the 88,000 people of French Polynesia, there are some people of mixed blood. There are also almost 10,000 Chinese, and about 2,000 Europeans, mostly French. The Chinese hold an important place in French Polynesia. They operate stores, even on the small islands. Sometimes the Chinese are bankers. Since Chinese, more often than Polynesians, get good educations, they are also accountants and bookkeepers.

Over 90 percent of the people are Christians, with more Protestants than Catholics. It is interesting that the Mormon Church has many members in French Polynesia, especially in the Tuomotu Islands. The French-Catholic fathers arrived on a small island in 1774. They were Father Geronimo Clota and Father Maximo Gonzales.

The Polynesians were more friendly to European explorers than were the Fijians. Missionary work was successful in a few years. In fact the first Christian missionaries to visit the Fiji Islands were Tahitians. Before the arrival of missionaries, the Polynesians worshiped stone gods. They had holy places called *maraes*. A marae is a great pile of stones and rocks. Most of these are now in poor repair.

Like the Melanesians, the Polynesians probably came from Southeast Asia and the islands of Indonesia. It is thought that they arrived in the Society Islands about 1300 A.D. Tahiti, Bora Bora, and Raiatea were the main islands settled by the Polynesians, and then other parts of the Pacific were settled from these islands. People sailing north arrived in and settled our Hawaiian Islands. Those sailing south came to New Zealand and were the ancestors of the Maori people of that country.

French Settlement and Government

The Marquesas were discovered in 1595 by a Spanish ship. In 1616, two Dutch navigators, Le Maire and Shouten, sailed through the Tuamotu Islands. Captain Samuel Wallis, an Englishman, discovered Tahiti in 1767. We have already read about Captain Cook's visit to Tahiti in 1769, and the famous voyage of the *Bounty* which stopped at Tahiti in 1789.

French possession of the Society Islands came about because of disagreement between Catholic and Protestant missionaries. As we have read, eighteen Protestant missionaries from the ship *Duff* landed in 1797, and were soon successful in their work. In 1836, two French Catholic fathers, Fathers Laval and Carret, came to Tahiti. After a short time they were expelled by the ruling queen.

The French Government was displeased and sent warships to Tahiti to demand money in payment for the bad treatment of the Catholic priests. Queen Pomare of Tahiti appealed to England for help. But just as the English were unwilling to help King Cakobau of Fiji when he offered

Queen Pomare's Tomb on Tahiti

MACKENZIE

to give his islands to them in exchange for help, so they were unwilling to help the Tahitians. In 1840, the French took control of the Marquesas Islands. Two years later Queen Pomare of Tahiti agreed to a French protectorate.

The next ruler of Tahiti was King Pomare V. The Society Islands remained under French protection for a number of years. But in 1880, the king was forced to cede the islands to the French. The Society Islands and the other island groups have belonged to France since that time. French Polynesia is not a colony, but is called an *Overseas Territory* of France.

There is a territorial assembly which meets in Papeete, the capital, and which has representatives from all the major islands. The members are elected by popular vote. The assembly has the power to determine the amount of money to be spent each year. It passes most of the laws about internal affairs in the islands.

We can see that the people of French Polynesia have more voice in their government than do Fijians. No native Polynesian pays taxes. Eighty-five percent of the land is owned by Polynesians, and it is very difficult for a Frenchman or any other outsider to buy land.

We learned that there is no free education in the Fiji Islands. In French Polynesia, all children go to schools, which are free. All children — French, Polynesian or Chinese — attend the same schools. French is the official language, and almost everyone can speak French .

The Tahitian language is still used by people in everyday affairs. Because Hawaii was populated by Polynesians who came from the Society Islands, it is not surprising that there are many similarities in language between the two groups of islands.

Tahitian is quite an easy language to learn. There are 13 letters in the alphabet, most of which are vowels. Let's learn a few Tahitian words and phrases.

How are you? is Maita'i oe? pronounced My-tah-EE-oh ay

Good-bye is Parahi, pronounced pah-RAH-hee
One is ho'e, pronounced HOH-ay
Two is piti, pronounced PEE-tee
Three is toru, pronounced TOH-roo

As we know, there were no written languages in the South Pacific. Even today, except for the Bible, there is almost nothing written in the Tahitian language. Books, newspapers and magazines are all written in French, and all school children study French. Both French and English words have been added to the language. For instance, the word *moni* (moe-Nee) is used for money.

How Polynesians Live

We have learned that Polynesians are different in appearance from Melanesians. There are also many differences in the way people live. The largest islands in French Polynesia are high and new islands. This means that the mountains are high; often peaks are jagged with high cliffs. No roads lead into the interior of Tahiti, Moorea or Bora Bora.

All the people live along the ocean shores, and there are no villages, as in the Fiji Islands. Instead, houses are strung out all along the one road that usually goes around or part way around an island. Many Polynesians still live in mud houses with thatched roofs, but many more now have houses of wood with corrugated tin roofs.

Each large island is divided into districts which are super-

Even small children learn the tamure.

vised by chiefs. However, district chiefs are now chosen in elections, and the people of a village do not hold their chiefs in the worshipful kind of respect that the Fijians do.

The food of most Polynesians is much like that of Fijians. Breadfruit, bananas, taro and tapioca are all eaten cooked. The lagoons have many fish, as well as other kinds of sea food.

A Tahitian feast is called a *tamaaraa* (tah-mah-ah-RAH-ah) and is a time of fun for children and adults. The feast begins when the people make a big fire in a pit. As the fire burns, stones are piled upon it. When the stones have become red hot, the Tahitian oven is ready for use. A whole suckling pig, pieces of fish, bananas, taro and breadfruit, are

85

placed on the hot rocks and covered with a thick layer of banana leaves. Another layer of leaves is placed over the banana leaves, and the food is left to cook for two or three hours.

Everyone who helps prepare the feast and everyone who eats it wears a garland of flowers around his head. The food is eaten with the fingers, and there is almost always singing and music with the feast.

Except for special occasions and dances, people dress more or less in western style. Most women wear a *pareu* (pah-RAY-oo). This is a long piece of brightly colored cotton cloth wrapped around the body from chest to knees. Boys and girls, men and women, often tuck a flower into their hair or behind an ear. Everyone love flowers. When a newcomer arrives or an old friend leaves, a *lei* (pronounced LAY) is placed around the neck of the honored person. This custom is common in Honolulu but originated in Tahiti. One time I saw a man at the Papeete airport with over one hundred leis around his neck!

When Europeans discovered the islands, they noticed that people greeted each other by rubbing noses. This custom is no longer followed. Instead, people kiss one another on both cheeks. This is a French custom which the Polynesians follow on every possible occasion.

It is interesting that tattooing originated in Tahiti. The first Europeans found both men and women decorated with indelible designs on their arms. The tattooing was done by pricking the arm with a piece of sharp bone dipped in a mixture of coconut oil and soot.

A New England ship's captain is said to have given Tahiti something that has become a problem — its mosquitoes. The captain had an argument with some Tahitians, and decided to get even. One night he took ashore a rotten water cask filled with mosquito eggs and larvae. The mosquitoes hatched and have done well in their new home ever since.

The most common bird on Tahiti and Moorea also came from abroad. It is the mynah bird which, as we have learned, is also abundant in the Fiji Islands. It is thought that mynah birds were brought by the Chinese. There are few native birds, and no native animals except the bats.

Farming and Fishing

The islands of French Polynesia are either small and flat or very rugged. There is not enough flat ground for big farms and plantations. Each family may have its small plot of taro or tapioca. There may be a few banana trees, or the family may get its bananas from the wild trees that grow in the hills.

As in most South Pacific Islands, copra is the most important product. Coconut palms grow along the shores of every island. On the next page is a picture of a small coconut plantation. Can you see the tin bands around each tree? According to law, all coconut trees must be banded in this manner.

The tin bands on the coconut palms are a health measure

to help stamp out a disease called elephantiasis. This disease is caused by a tiny parasite that gets into the blood of people through the bites of mosquitoes. Unless a coconut palm is banded with a strip of tin, rats climb up and eat holes in the young coconuts. Then the nuts fall to the ground, and after rains, the little holes are filled with water. Mosquitoes lay their eggs in the stagnant water in the coconuts.

Elephantiasis, the disease which makes the legs swell up to an enormous size, is disappearing now. Modern medicine and the banding of the coconut palms have helped to do away with this sickness as well as with malaria, another disease carried by mosquitoes.

In addition to coconuts, the islands grow small amounts of coffee and cocoa. And French Polynesia is second in importance to the West Indies in the production of vanilla.

A coconut plantation

AUTHOR

This popular flavoring comes from the pods or beans of a variety of orchid. The plants are grown on poles, somewhat as are string beans.

Each vanilla flower must be pollinated by hand, and people call this process "marrying the vanilla." After picking, the long beans are dried and then shipped to other countries. Perhaps the vanilla in our ice cream comes from faraway Tahiti or Moorea.

We have learned that Fijians, for the most part, use boats with motors. Outrigger canoes are found only on the outlying islands. In French Polynesia, the outrigger canoe is still found everywhere. Often an outboard motor may be used to push the canoe, but sails and paddles are still used by many people.

Since almost every family lives near the ocean, fish is an important food. It is an unusual family that does not have an outrigger canoe to use for fishing, for visiting friends, or for going to the Chinese store, which may be several miles away.

There are big fish in the deep waters outside the barrier reefs. There are also many fish that may be caught by nets within the lagoons. Or fish may be speared. Spearfishing takes place in shallow lagoon water. The fisherman stands very still until a big fish swims near. Then he throws the long, sharp-pointed spear at the fish.

Very few people ever go hungry in Polynesia. We might say that there are always fish in the front yard. And in the back yard there are breadfruit, bananas and taro.

A Visit to Papeete

Tahiti is only 37 miles long, shaped like the figure 8, with one part of the 8 much larger than the other. The island was formed when two volcanoes erupted from the sea and joined together at a narrow place called the Isthmus of Taravao. Papeete is located at the western end of the large part of the 8. The beautiful island of Moorea is 9 miles away from Papeete.

Half of the population of French Polynesia lives on Tahiti; and almost half of Tahiti lives in Papeete, which has a population of 20,000. The city is situated on a lagoon. There is a break in the barrier reef through which big ships can pass. The harbor is filled with schooners that visit other islands to take supplies or collect copra. There are nearly always American yachts that have sailed from as far away as New England.

The streets of Papeete are filled with vehicles. In the mornings almost all stores close for two and a half hours at 11:30; and if you were to visit Papeete at this hour, you would think the whole island was on wheels. There are hundreds of bicycles, motor bikes with small motors attached above the front wheels, and motor scooters. Office girls ride their bikes, motor bikes or scooters, to and from work. Mothers go to the market on their bikes, often carrying small children with them.

There are almost 15,000 two-wheeled vehicles on Tahiti. There are also several thousand cars and trucklike buses called *jitneys*. The jitneys are painted in gay colors and are given names. Passengers may carry fish, chickens, bunches of bananas or breadfruit. Often there are no regular stops. When the driver sees a freshly cut coconut frond across the highway, he knows that someone wants to be picked up.

The road around Tahiti is only 100 miles in length. With so many bikes, motor bikes and jitneys, it always seems crowded. Other islands have so few roads that there are only a handful of vehicles on them, but the motor bike or motor scooter is always the most popular family vehicle.

Songs, Dances and Legends

The people of Tahiti and the other Society Islands are often called the gayest and most carefree people in the world. Because of the friendly people and the pleasant climate, many foreigners have gone to Tahiti to visit and have never returned home. This has become a problem to the French Government. Now no outsider may visit the islands unless he has a round-trip ticket back to his home.

All the South Pacific islanders like to sing and dance. The Polynesians love most to dance the *tamure* (tah-mur-e) which is something like the Twist. Men and women, boys and girls, all learn to shake their hips to gay guitar music. The music of Polynesia is much like that of Hawaii. Of course we know now that the original Hawaiians came from the Society Islands. Hawaiian music is really Polynesian music.

Islanders like to dress as they did when the Europeans first arrived, and to spend a whole evening dancing. The women wear grass skirts, the men colorful *maros* (mar-os) or loin cloths. With the instrumental music, there is always singing and handclapping.

Many of the Polynesian dances and songs tell stories and legends of the past. The Canoe Dance of Moorea Island and the song which accompanies the dance tell the story of how the South Pacific Islands were populated. The dancers, men and women, sit on the ground and go through the motions of paddling a double-decker canoe. Seated in the middle are the chief and his wife. A man standing at the rear makes motions as if he were steering the canoe.

The canoe song is sad at first as it tells the story of a tribe forced to move when its island home becomes too crowded. Then, as a new and beautiful island is sighted the movements become faster and the song happier. As the canoe reaches the beach all the sorrow is gone, and the singers tell the story of going ashore to establish a new home.

The canoe dance and song tell the story of how the South Pacific Islands were actually reached and settled. There are other songs that tell other stories of the past. Some dances and songs are common to all the islands of Polynesia. Often there are legends that have to do only with one island or group of islands. Much of what we know about the history of the island people comes from the songs and dances of people who had no written language with which to record their history.

In this book we have been able only to visit a few of the South Pacific Islands. Until recently, few Americans were able to visit the islands. But now cruise ships take thousands of tourists to Tahiti and to the Fiji Islands. Jet planes fly nonstop from Los Angeles to Papeete, and from Honolulu to Nadi Airport in the Fiji Islands.

Other islands are still visited by only a few outsiders. We have not had space to tell about Samoa, an American Territory of 76 square miles, with a population of 21,000 Polynesians. The nearby islands of Western Samoa are much larger, and in 1962 became the only independent nation in the South Pacific.

As airplane transportation becomes faster, and as more and more people are able to travel, the many islands of the South Pacific will become better known. Island people, who in many cases were bloodthirsty cannibals one hundred years ago, are now among the friendliest people in the world. Outsiders who visit the islands learn to love them and their peoples, just as Robert Louis Stevenson did many years ago. Stevenson lived at Tautira on Tahiti at first, then moved on to Samoa, where he died.

The people of Samoa called Stevenson *Tusitala,* or "Teller of Tales." When he died, sixty Samoans carried his body to the top of Mount Vaea, where he was buried, and on his gravestone were carved the words which he himself had written:

UNDER THE WIDE AND STARRY SKY
DIG THE GRAVE AND LET ME LIE.
GLAD DID I LIVE AND GLADLY DIE,
   AND I LAID ME DOWN WITH A WILL.
THIS BE THE VERSE YOU GRAVE FOR ME:
"HERE HE LIES WHERE HE LONGED TO BE;
HOME IS THE SAILOR, HOME FROM THE SEA,
   AND THE HUNTER HOME FROM THE HILL."

ABOUT THE AUTHOR

John C. Caldwell was born in the Orient and went to school there before coming to the United States to attend college.

Mr. Caldwell went to South China during World War II and spent fifteen months behind the Japanese lines on the China coast. After the war he was transferred to the Department of State and held various positions in a program which has since become known as the United States Information Service.

Since he began writing, Mr. Caldwell has traveled regularly to gather material. He has crossed the Pacific 37 times, the Atlantic 8 times, and has traveled throughout Asia, South America and Africa. He is the author of the *Far East Travel Guide* and the *South Asia Travel Guide* for adults as well as the *Let's Visit* series and *World Neighbors* series for children. Before writing *Let's Visit the South Pacific* he made a special trip to that area in 1962.

Index